GW01080106

ANCHOR BOOKS

NATURAL PEACE

First published in Great Britain in 1995 by
ANCHOR BOOKS
1-2 Wainman Road, Woodston,
Peterborough, PE2 7BU

All Rights Reserved

Copyright Contributors 1995

SB ISBN 1 85930 038 3

Foreword

Anchor Books is a small press, established in 1992, with the aim of promoting readable poetry to as wide an audience as possible.

We hope to establish an outlet for writers of poetry who may have struggled to see their work in print.

The poems presented here have been selected from many entries. Editing proved to be a difficult and daunting task and as the Editor, the final selection was mine.

The poems chosen represent a cross-section of styles and content. They have been sent from all over the world, written by young and old alike, united in the passion for writing poetry.

I trust this selection will delight and please the authors and all those who enjoy reading poetry.

Andrew Head
Editor

CONTENTS

A GARDEN OF DREAMS . . .

What are we left with when a dream becomes Reality?
When the garden of the mind reaches its ripeness
Should we prune, take cuttings, encouraging new growth,
Or do we lay it to waste -
Heaping our work into a corner -
And start anew?
Should we tend what we have, lovingly and lastingly,
Training each leaf and tendril to our heart's desire,
Or reassess with the passing seasons
The burgeoning, or fading glories of each flower and tree?
Dreams are like plants;
Some grow to majestic proportions in one short season,
And then are dead.
Others take a lifetime to develop -
They are slow - growing,
But becoming ever more magnificent with the passing years -
Monumental wonders,
For future generations to enjoy, take seed from -
Or to cut down . . .
Destroy not my dreams, for they are my lifetime's glory,
Late-germinating, and developing,
But ever-lasting in their flowering,
With roots deep-sunk, and far-spreading -
Invisible -
But for ever holding up, and nurturing
The Realities you see before you.
My words and works
Have been the blossoming of the Dream - Time of my soul . . .
A garden of dreams, from the late-flowering of my mind.

J Margaret Service

1

SPRING

First I saw some snowdrops
Then crocuses so gay
I knew that golden daffodils
Would soon be on their way
Flowering trees in blossom
Then hyacinths that cheer
Primulas, narcissi
And tulips will appear
Standing tall like sentinels
The message that they bring
Is that Winter's over
They're heralds that it's Spring

Sheila Phelan

AUTUMN

As we walk through leafy lanes
The signs are all around,
Sunny days are on the wane
As autumn tints abound,
Watery sun through branches glinting
And the shortening Day's dying fruits
on cobwebbed bushes, and the misty haze,
Paths and hedges all around us, silent
seem to be, but nature's furred and
Feathered creatures work with great activity,
Here the busy squirrels forage,
Laying in their winter store, beach nuts, Acorns,
Seeds and grasses, these they will retrieve
Once more, from the place where they are hidden
When the snowy fields are raw. Little hedgehogs
Too, are searching, for, a place where they retire,
There to sleep the sleep of winter, maybe in the
Farmyard byre. Tiny field mice seeking warmth
Now, try to find a cosy fire.
In the trees the birds are gathering life's long
Journey to begin, over mighty seas and mountains
As migration calls to them, but one friend the
Cheeky robin, through the winter will remain,
Chirruping on snowy mornings tapping on the
Window Panes. He is with us through the seasons
Until springtime comes again

Sheila Town

THE MECHANICAL AGE

Once it was men and machines
Now it is machines and men
Taking over men's work
      and everything it seems!
The press button age
making everything run smoothly?
Progress it is called
But now there's too much
Taking away adventure
      and people's feelings as such
Destruction of nature
      and all its resources
A nation of robots conceived
      from all the world's forces
The end of governments
      and all that entails
The dignity of man and the beauty
      of Nature
All gone when all else fails!
      God help us! A future Robot

J W Wight

THE ROSES

Standing tall and bright,
making our drab table a pretty sight.

Delicate petals of silk they seem -
droplets of water making them gleam.

A delicate beauty they seem to hold,
a personality that can only be described
as bold.

It is all to easy for them to die -
for that it is the only thing about
roses that makes me want to cry

Emma Broomfield

TREES

Wintry trees, reach for the sky,
Lost their leaves, but they don't cry
They stand up tall, through it all,
Winter, spring, summer and fall.
A world without trees would never please,
How would we hear the cool summer breeze,
Or children playing in autumn leaves
They bring about a sense of calm,
In this world full of fury, destruction and harm
Their quiet strength and beauty, creates a stillness is one's soul,
But they're not seeing how everything is getting so out of control
Let me shelter at your bough,
Contemplate, think awhile,
Your secret power on this earth.
Being taken for granted for all it's worth.
Let us stop, take time out,
Ask ourselves what it's all about,
Realise, there is a price to pay.
When we do our own thing, go our own way,
Destroying something so precious.
Can you not see,
The importance of nature,
For you and for me.
So when you have finished with your technology and progress,
Let's hope it doesn't finish us in the process
Because there will come a time
When you will not need it,
But let us hope that there will
Still be trees for our children to
Sit under, grass for our children
To play on and for our children's children.

So let us stop and take time out,
Ask ourselves what it's all about,
Make some choices, share and prepare,
In our world for survival,
We all must care.

Michelle O'Flaherty

AUTUMN

Summer surrenders to Autumn, another year matures and weakens its hold,
Trees stand resplendent in their seasonal colours, bejewelled in finest amber
and gold
Startling yellow leaves dance in the breeze like flames in a fire,
Beacons, illuminating dull grey days, warming the soul,

Oceans of deep grey clouds roll along as a celestial tide across the sky,
Smothering God's earth with an impenetrable dampness,
Cooling and watering sun parched soil, lulling into winter's sleep.
Marking time, lest we forget our mortality.

Chattering assemblies of migrating birds, frenzied excitement reaching
its peak
Permeating spent summer skies; time to go.
Who tells you so? The cold that chills tiny bones
Mysterious far away destinations I have never seen
Take me with you, let my spirit soar on your wings

Roofscape silhouettes deplete; teaming skies become silent,
Leaving us to our winter. A faithful few break rank,
To relieve our chilly solitude.
Return with haste little ones bringing with you spring.

J T Malone

THE RETREAT

We lay in bed one Summer's eve
And gazed on sea and sky,
Seagulls' screams heard overhead
And boats were passing by.

The fisherman's cottage we had hired
Was snug and tidy-clean,
The clear sea air and magic scene
Was all one could desire.

On cliff-buff top its weathered stones
Stood stark above the chine,
A sentinel so proud, so grand,
Its watchful gaze o'er sea and sand
Portrayed the scars of time.

The foaming surf so far below
E'er constant in its surge,
Brought thoughts of sons and fathers gnarled,
By tempest's cruellest scourge.

Some lobster pots, a few draped nets
And yellowy oil-skin coats,
A catch so lean for toil extreme
Around lone up-turned boats.

An artist eyed a sunset dream
His brush could not portray,
A shimmered sea, so calm, serene,
So crimson o'er the bay.

The shoulders of the sea, bore, last traces of the sun
And darkness in its stealth crept up,
Of a sudden, the light was gone.

J R Hutchinson

NATURE

They call them the old masters
        their well known paintings on display.
I know the originals of their workings
        for I see them every day.

My master paints for me a sunrise
        he plays sweet music every dawn
I hear his birds a singing
        'Arise my child, tis morn'

He can change his brush with seasons
        from Autumn to winter then spring
He knows I like the summer the best.
        for tis then my heart takes wing

The balmy nightly for walking
        the days of lying in the sun.
I like the rest, seasons in time
        but my heart the summer's won.

This year I'll have a look at Springtime
        watch the plants and flowers take form.
Will they quiver like I as they stir into life
        and reach their leaves to the sun who is warm.

Rosie Hues

NADULTERATED

Is there anything like seeing
A world that is fresh and clean?
The clear blue sky,
The quiet mountain stream,
The sun-dappled path
That runs through the wood,
The golden haired daisy,
The breeze that feels good,
The rambling weeds that many have hated,
I see it lying unadulterated,
Heals my heart, restores my sight,
Above me still the sun shines bright,
And as I turn myself to go,
I know it must remain pure.

Ruth Calder

THE ELEMENTS

The winds they shriek and they rage,
Like wild demented animals trapped in a cage,
Trying to pull roots away from the earth,
The winds blowing and gusting for all their worth,
Blowing harder and harder than before,
Increasing in strength to blow some more,
Anything stands within its wake,
It's not there long, in a thousand pieces it will break,
Nothing will stand the ferocity of the wind
Within its wake the rains it will bring
Now they are one the rain and the wind
Delivering yet another sting
The rain bounces off roofs and paths
While the wind looks on and laughs
The thunder awakens with a loud clap
Rain lashes down harder like water from a tap
A fork of lightning tears across the night
And things which are not battered down grow wings and take flight
These four are now a team the thunder and lightning the wind and rain
And now the biggest of them all a hurricane
It comes in in a frenzy a right angry strop
And when it's quenched its anger that's when it will stop.

John Rea

TREES ARE LIKE PEOPLE

Trees are like people
Some straight, some tall,
Some are quite gnarled
And some very small.
But each has a beauty
However they grow,
Shelter for the sparrow,
As well as the crow.
Some are very strong,
Some are quite brittle,
But it matters not
If they are big, or little.
They each have a beauty
All of their own.
Some need company,
While others stand alone,
So, whether it's people, or trees
That happen your way,
Give them a smile,
And wish them 'Good Day'

Sandy Cracknell

THE WOODLAND AT DAWN

The rays of sunshine slanted through the trees
And lit the pathways up with floods of light.
The angled branches silhouetted now
Gave added beauty to this wondrous sight.

The ferns were tinted golden in the sun.
The ground untrodden by the day ahead
Was carpeted with softly fallen leaves
In lovely shades of yellow, brown and red.

The air was sweet and pure this new born day.
Its freshness brought a sense of peace to me.
Alone yet never lonely, I just felt
Such meaning, that my eyes could never see.

Nor was I just alone, within this wood
Grey squirrels, rabbits too, came near.
While I stood still, they scurried to and fro.
They sensed I was a friend and showed no fear.

I went back later but the scene had changed.
The carpets and the pathways now were trod.
There'd be another dawn, another day
To know with joy the greatness of our God.

John Christopher Cole

14

AUTUMN

Now the leaves are turning brown,
Soon they'll all come fluttering down,
Days grow short, and nights are long,
Soon we'll hear no sweet birds song,

Misty mornings now are here,
Cold at first, then warm and clear,
Evenings chill, then home we go
To the fireside's cheerful glow.

WINTER

Icicles form, and gale winds blow,
Winter is here again,
The branches are bare, the fields are brown,
Whirling snowflakes dance around,
Silently cover the ground.

Cold crispy days, and frosty nights,
Winter is here again.
The stars come out, the moon shines bright,
All earth sleeps in Winter white,
Waiting for warmth and for light.

Pamela Stoner

WHITE RABBITS!

Rain-spattered panes affront the sleep-dimmed eyes,
A chill envelopes one's very being.
Too soon for lighted windows -
December's here - night's slumbers intrude into the day.

Headlights appear in the village,
Jostling bottles and crates herald the milkman,
A whistled tune carries on the still-dusk air,
Wisps of vapour make their way from mouth to lamplight.

Chinks of light appear from home to home.
Breakfasts, hastily swallowed, greet the day,
Soon bairns are jostled off to school.
Scarlet and white, gold and green flash down the lane.

Pete's on his way - tractor piled with hay.
He should have lights - but we all know he's there!
Quadrille waits by the gate - eager to take his share.

The stillness of the village an hour before, has vanished, all is now astir.
Judy is abroad - her string of dogs straining at the leash.
It's light now, though drear and dull -
But somehow animation lifts the gloom.

Not-quite zombies drive their cars to work.
Buckets scrape their way to outside taps.
Cattle low in their stalls to greet the day.
Cats dart from their nooks to brimming bowls.

Three weeks to Christmas! We'll dress the tree!
We'll deck the house with holly - the beams with lights!
And when we go to bed we'll leave the drapes
Then dancing cheer will be for all to see.

Ernie will put the village tree in his garden.
The lights will shine all night
We'll stare in wonder, as we do from year to year -
Ever delighting in the joys we share.

The clock is lit upon the church,
Eleanor's tree will light the window in the shop.
The pub will soon declare 'Merry Christmas' -
And we won't care that it rains - or even snows - we'll keep on top!

Frances Alder

PRELUDE TO SPRING

It is cold this winter's morn
The wind so rough, my sheets nearly torn
So many years I have lived on this hill
Each day the currents can stand my body still
I love this plot each season of the year
Always something different causing me to stare
The robin comes and books his patch
Soon the blackbirds in the hedge will hatch
Their babies so ugly look up and stare
Never knowing if the cat is anywhere near
He stalks along the hedgerow so thick
Just wondering if there is a lunch he can easily pick
Nature is so cruel sometimes we know
It would be nice if those birds could grow
Lilting their voices in the morning air
When summer is here, and the trees no longer bare.

Gladys Brighty

FLOWER POWER

Tall splendour of sunflowers, red roses in bloom
Delicately laced ferns, swaying in the breeze
Tossing away my anxiety and gloom
Spiky red hot pokers, pink blossom trees

Scent of the lilacs and lavender blue
Majestic iris, beside yellow daffodils
Mottled red tulips, cornflowers blue
Spring, summer favourites, that grow by the mill

R Humphrey

THE SCARLET MOOR

The heather shines upon the moor,
    And tinkles like stray bells,
That rustle in the tempest's roar,
    As clouds above them swell.

A coat of scarlet covering,
    The bones of Scottish dead,
That ache to raise a Scottish King,
    Though Charlie's long since fled.

And as the clouds unveil the moon,
    Strange wisps of shadows walk
And through it all a piper's tune,
    Drifts on the air like smoke.

A flash of blade, a swish of kilt,
    The howl of Scottish throats,
A stream of hot blood freshly spilt
    From hearts of young redcoats.

Then all is calm upon the moor,
    And silence reigns again.
The scarlet heather aye endures,
    The moor of Culloden.

James Shillito

TIMID LIFE

Fidgety mouse cheeky and small
exploring my world,
Through a hole in the wall.

Searching for crumbs
On the kitchen floor.
Rushing and hiding,
under the door

Grey furry mammal,
with petite toes,
Your whiskers flicker,
at the end of your nose.

Those shinny eyes
no bigger than beads,
Wafer thin ears,
teeth nibble with ease.

Tiny and sensitive,
why so shy?
Your heart beats fast,
as I walk by.

Warm body trembling
You scurry away,
Your watching for danger,
both night and day.

Shy little creature,
with babies so small,
you hurry home quickly,
to comfort them all.

Frightened and timid,
Your babies so young,
with lives always threatened,
Your works never done.

Christine Hulett

THE CRUEL WORLD

I see some pointed ears,
then a bushy tail flies by.
Suddenly, I realise,
as I hear that painful cry.
A fox is getting hunted,
for trying to live his life,
for feeding all his children,
and his loving wife.
He's the stealthiest of hunters,
while catching his waiting prey
But now he's getting hunted
and he's trying to get away.
His thick red coat is heavy,
and is dragging on the ground.
Now he's running faster,
as he hears that dreadful sound,
of the guns which are getting closer
and the dogs who are after him.
What are they doing this for?
He has committed no sin.
I hear a cry 'The fox is dead'!
Now some cheers of glee
Nobody thinks of the other things;
his home and his family.
What will become of them now
with no-one to stand guard
They'll live in fear of getting hunted
Their lives will become hard.

Jenny Beattie

WONDER AND DESPAIR

Ebb and flow, ebb and flow,
Oh waves, why do you come and go
Just when I think I know your ways,
You change again!

Ebb and flow,
They say it's the moon,
But I often wonder,
Can it be so?

Quiet and still, quiet and still,
Oh waves what makes you so?
Roll and roar or smooth and calm,
I watch you run with a hiss up the shore.

Tomorrow's eve
Your path of silver
Draws me again.
Is it the path that leads to peace?

Ebb and flow, ebb and flow,
Oh waves,
What shall I find if I rise and follow?

W Kershaw

THE BRAVE INDIAN

Here . . .
Upon these high dry plains I see
Deep valleys flowing endlessly
The golden ground with sunkissed land
Where wind and rain both lend a hand
My breath is wind and ground is bed
And ere' here shall I lay my head
Where once I walked with earthly feet
To where the earth and sky do meet
And saw my fellow clansmen live
With nature here and all she give . . .

Together . . .
We'd hunt and track the bear and deer
and buffalo, with lance and spear
To feed my daughter and my son
and wear their skins when warmth was gone
These giant beast now wander still
O'er sacred plains and drink their fill
From crystal waters flowing where
the wolf is friendly with the bear.

And never was a life to waste
For days were full and quickly paced
The work went on for one and all
From tiny child to man so tall
Through youthful spring 'till ageing fall . . .

We saw sweet nature work so hard
And so we joined to share the load
The bounty of our land was fair
Together! Meant we all could share
Throughout our tribes across the plains
And still our fire and love remains
Our bodies may be all be gone
But forever will our souls walk on.

Upon these high dry plains I see
These valleys flowing endlessly . . .

Sarah Bond

COUNTRY SUMMER FEELING

I leave for you a legacy
Of hazy summer sky,
Of pansies in a window box,
The smiles of passers by,
Hollyhocks and lupins,
Foxgloves, tall and gay,
Roses and clematis,
The scent of new mown hay.
An English lane in Springtime,
A Blackbird in her nest,
Contented summer cattle,
Laying down to rest,
The buzzing of the honey bee
On the 'suckle by the door,
Cucumber, and strawberries,
And cake for tea at four . . .

Barbara Huffey

ROBIN COMES VISITING

I was sitting at my window
While the snow fell thick and fast
The apple tree was white with frost,
The sky was overcast.

Out of the dark grey clouds there came
As swift as he could fly
A happy little robin
With a merry, twinkling eye.

He perched upon my window sill,
And most politely said;
(in whistly robin- language)
'Please, can you spare some bread'
I gave him crumbs of bread and scone
You should have heard the song he sang
To thank me then, my dears
I don't think I'll forget it
If I live a hundred years.

Ivy O Eastwick

AUTUMN TREES

The trees stand tall braving all,
Leaves are gold when they fall,
It's not the end but just the start,
Of a new beginning for one and all,
The land is fed from gold above,
Only if you knew it was sent with love,
When the spring returns again,
We can harvest fruits,
That grow above,
Harvest the land,
Where leaves did fall,
Because it was given for one and all.

Linda Semmens

HOME OF THE WILDLIFE?

So many things I'd like to say
I just can't find the words
I can't express the happiness
They bring to me . . . *the birds.*

So many different colours
So many different songs
So many different habits
So many have all gone!

Because of greed *(not need)*
The human race destroys
An ever decreasing countryside
Where *all* wildlife resides.

Graham Dennis

SUMMER TIME

Summer time is on its way,
And in the sun we all still play,
Mother Nature starts things to grow,
She takes her time, sometimes slow,
Creatures from their sleep do wake,
After their long winter break,
Fur and feathers they start to preen,
So at their best they can be seen,
Things look better in the sun,
Already the spring cleaning should be done,
We all start to set and sow,
People all over are on the go,
Summer salads will soon be had,
A nice cool drink will make you glad,
So in the morning summer dew,
Just take your time and enjoy the view.

Clem

A PEBBLE

I'm a little pebble
I live upon a beach
Every now and then I'm thrown right out of reach
I'm skimmed across the water
I'm buried in the sand
And sometimes a little boy
Will hold me tightly in his hand
I'm a little pebble
I live upon the beach
I have no eyes and no hair
I'm round flat and sleek
I like it when you pick me up
And skim me across the sea
Whee! Hee! Here I go up in the air
Jumping one, two, three
Plop I'm down under the waves
I'll be here for a little while
I'll have to wait till the tide goes in
And then I'll travel back in style
Until then I'll have a little snooze
Deep down on the sea floor
When I awake I'll be ready
To skim some more and more.

Ruth Davies

31

THE ELDERLY CATERPILLAR

A summer fayre in mid July,
coloured pennants against the sky.
My mind a blur as sleep moves in
fondest memories of distant kin.
One last thought before I die

The fresh smell of an autumn breeze,
that harvest pollen the wind did tease.
Those muggy nights when all was calm
mother nature's power, such tender charm.
One last thought before I die.

Now as I cling to this fragile frame
and dream of days too numerous to name,
the winter's wind cuts like a knife
at last to sleep but lust for life.
One last thought before I die.

And as I stretch my new found wings,
remembering nothing of bygone things.
I flit and fly over hill and dale
bouncing along on a late spring gale.
One may realise that I did not die
I became a *butterfly*

Alex I Askaroff

MAY

Blessed are they who are born in May, the
  loveliest month of the year.
When all of England is green and fresh
  and skies are bright and clear.
When chestnuts in splendour bloom
  and lilacs everywhere
In ancient, cottage gardens, will perfume
  the balmy air.

Beneath them grow blue irises, the
  pinks and paenies,
And way up high, young thrushes sing from
  flowering hawthorn trees.
Go wandering in the woodlands, where
  anemones can be found,
And vast seas of nodding bluebells, grow
  carpeting the ground.

In May the young men's thoughts are turned
  to love, and girls, to kiss
But all the winter, girls have had
  romantic dreams of this.
When rough March winds are long forgot
  and April showers are past,
Then comes this merry month of May, and
  spring-time's here, at last.

Joan Adams

SNOW

As brilliant as diamonds snow flutters to rest
Covering the scape with a crispness and zest
A beautiful picture is cast overnight
Curtains are opened to this shivering sight
Tranquillity displayed like a fairytale scene
Like a looking glass shows it reflects the sun's gleam
But this angelic shade is just a disguise
Sent from the heavens to hinder our lives
The problems so caused by this innocent show
Are to take many lives who would think this of snow
It barricades cities communications are down
Is there life in the next village city or town
Predicted to fall but precautions are none
The roads are not gritted the salt has all gone
Winds drift it so deep no use to go out
The heavens must think mankind needs a clout
Loved by the young for the sun that it holds
Deplored by the old and for its life stopping cold
The verdict for snow some good but most bad
The only purpose it serves is to make us all sad

Gary Paul Clarke

THE STORM

Listen to the wind, it's raising very high,
Black clouds are rolling, across a moonlit sky
Great trees are bending, taking on the strain,
Creatures run for cover, from the expected rain,
The twinkling stars, no longer shine so proud,
The moon gently smothered by a blanket of dark cloud,
Thunder can be heard, it rolls and then it crashes,
Followed by lightning with bright running flashes,
It's right above and has travelled very quick,
The air feels warm and gotten quite thick,
A roll of thunder goes ripping through the air,
Louder and louder, it seems to have no care,
With a fierce explosion, it turns night into day,
All I can do is lay down and pray,
That it's over very quickly, please let it be,
Because at this moment, it's frightening to me,
My prayers are answered as it swings out to the west,
At last, it's gone quiet, perhaps now I can rest?

R P Williams

WORKING TOGETHER

Our planet is dying, of that there's no doubt
And man has caused its fall.
To repair the damage that's been done
Should be the aim of us all.
Save the forests, save the whale,
Plug up the ozone layer,
Stop ivory poaching, protect wildlife,
Should be our communal prayer.
If we pull together, then man has a chance,
The earth will live again
But ignore the signs, show apathy,
Then we keep the pollution, the acid rain
Our seas stay polluted, our rivers run dry,
Together we stop the rot.
Working together is our only chance,
The only one we've got.
United we stand, divided we fall,
Together we can start a reversal.
We've only one life, we've only one world,
This is it - it's not a rehearsal.
All working together with one aim in sight,
A world reborn anew.
Reborn, rebuilt, replenished
By the likes of me and you:
Together we make the difference
Together we make our stand.
Together we win at the end of the day,
Soul to soul, heart to heart, hand in hand.

Theresa Miles

THE GRACEFUL SWAN

'Twas eventime and the sun was setting,
Casting its rays in a glorious netting
Of shimmering gems across the lake,
Encircling the swan as she did make
Her way across the rippling scene,
Silently, ghostly, as in a dream.

With watchful eye and neck so slender,
She glided by with graceful splendour,
Into the sunset, floating serenely,
With gleaming white plumage, lonely yet Queenly.
Dipping her neck in the rippling pool,
Haughty, but gracious, calmly and cool.

As the sun disappears way down in the west.
The beautiful swan returns to her nest,
As the darkness befalls, and the moon rises high,
A sprinkling of stars light up in the sky.
On her downy white back the swan nestles her head,
And blissfully sleeps in the warmth of her bed.

Edith M Smith

WINTER DREAMS

Have you ever been pretending
That it's summer once again
While taking a walk in winter
Being soaked by driving rain

As you stroll beside a sea-front
Listening to screaming gulls,
Being very close to nature
As you exercise your lungs

Your mind may start to wander
And you leave that windy shore,
Transported on a magic carpet
Far away from winter's woe

Life is grand if you are a dreamer
With a face never wearing a frown,
For you will be certain to have many friends
And will never let life get you down

Denzil Broadstock

BIRDS

Birds come as if from nowhere, some at
certain times make the air fill with magic
with their beautiful singing.

To watch them, when they have a bath either in
dust or water, to hear all their quarrelling, and
to see their beautiful colours quiet unbelievable
to behold.

The whistling of the blackbird, the thrush, and
the dear little robin, and many more, the
chortling of the starlings, the steady chirping
of the sparrow.

The homeward flocks darken the sky,
going all of them, in these days, I know not
where.

After all so many thickets, and hedges
keep disappearing to make room for homes
and industries of course the crops are sprayed.

We can all feel a little guilty, as we have
come to expect the best in food.

Therefore some of the disappearing birds can
be attributed to us all.

Jean Dickens

UNTITLED

Looking out of the window pane
Seeing the heavy deluge of rain
Dripping, making patterns anew
Trees swaying, the birds are few
Fluttering by
They fly
Looking for shelter
Clouds like a helter skelter
Now the trees perform a dance
Bare of leaves that used to prance
Swirling around
To the sound
The winds blow stronger
Howling, days growing longer
Soon the sky will get bright
Another day over, now it's night

Joye

MUSIC OF CHILDHOOD

So many sounds
            To make our hearts sing
Like the song of the birds
            That heralds the spring;
The humming of bees
            As for nectar they search,
The chiming of bells
            At the old village church;
The rippling stream
            As it trips on its way;
The melodious notes
            When the violins play;
The kettle that sings
            When it's put on for tea;
The chorus of gulls
            Telling tales of the sea;

But no sweeter sound
            My soul to beguile
Than the laughter that comes
            From the heart of a child.

Sarah Blackburn

SCOWLES

Who knows what deeds you've seen,
Deep pitted woodland acres.
Ancient scrabbling of man
Now mellowed and green.
Great boulders covered in moss
Trails of ivy hang
O'er cliffs and chasms left
by man's earliest quest for iron.
How many suffered and died?
Was there time to stop and ponder?
Twentieth century life gives me
time to imagine and wonder.
Unspoilt now by man's plunder.
The wild life abounds,
roots scarcely in the ground.
Tall beeches soar skyward
Yews hang at impossible angles,
Why don't they fall over?
Nestled deep in the root system
Sucking moisture from rock faces,
Clumps of leafy green ferns,
make the most of the sunshine.
e're the canopy returns.
As we stroll through these woodlands
enjoying freedom and health
Spare a thought for our forefathers
who created this scene.
Before the coal miners in the dark mists of time
Those who mined iron ore for the wealth of the King.

Louise McGuinness

COUNTRY SOUNDS

Country sounds have changed - subtly not the same
Since the chiff-chaff no longer chants his name
Or flamboyant cuckoo his repeated tone.
They have - like nightingales and warblers flown
South with swallows to a sunnier clime,
With instinctive flight from our winter-time.
Today I paused under a leafless tree,
The robin's winter song, in minor key,
Vied with the song thrush's cheerful trill
To dispel all thoughts of gloom and chill
And remind me that it won't be so long
Before I hear again the chiff-chaff's song,
When echoing cuckoos fly far and wide
Across the Somerset countryside.

Joy Mullins

A VIEW DOWN RIVER

Standing on the Clifton Downs,
staring into the Gorge below,
I have to catch my breath
as I see the Avon flow.
So far down beneath me,
sun shining over the water
making the river glow.
The dark green foliage of the bushy trees
looks so still in the cool summer breeze.
I watch the river disappear,
winding and bending all the time,
out into the cool and open seas.

Anthea Youens

UP THE DOWNS

Sweet summer smells hang still in the air
as the dappled warm sunlight caress skin and hair,
I lay on the grass beneath the oak trees
and listen to leaves dance in the breeze.

I feel the damp grass under my hand
and feel the warm texture of life giving land.
The butterflies flit, mosaics on show,
darting and diving across the meadow.

The blue of the sky, the white of the cloud,
the birds singing sweetly, dogs barking loud.
Echoing laughter, kids having fun,
mankind and nature both are as one.

But walk to the edge, just stand and stare,
at man's concrete creation, look at the glare.
The bustling madness, the noise and the strife,
of man's mindless meandering of modern day life.

Oasis of beauty are too hard to find
and soon will be memories in the back of the mind.
The creation of nature, man cannot compete,
so leave it alone, we need no more concrete.

J Jones

WINTERTIME

The season of decline,
decay,
an outlook bleak
a lean array.
A keen and biting wind
prevails,
cold hard land
with wintry gales.

A season gone to ground,
retreated,
inactive stillness
but not defeated.
Earth lies sleeping
in slumber waits,
a few more months
'til summer dates.

Karen Jones

SPRING IN THE CITY

Under pavements
Plane trees
Waking, yawn
And stretch their roots.

On doorsteps,
Cats
Blink in the sun:
Hymning their warm fur.

In cars,
Drivers
Done to a turn,
Frying like pink sausages.

In supermarkets
Checkouts
Lusting after housewives:
Smiles on offer.

In parks,
Cherry trees
Raining pink and daffodils
Dreaming of green fields.

Somewhere,
A thrush
Singing all this sweeter
And stronger than I can.

Jill Truman

AUTUMN AROUND THE SLAUGHTERS

Garden bonfires and apple-log smoke,
Bitter-sweet chrysanthemums and moulting oak,
Earwigs probing in dahlia petals,
Old men yearning on tavern settles.

Cassock and surplice strut of magpie,
Mummified plums beneath an embalmed sky;
Timorous bleat of reeking goats,
Wolds of whiskered barley and tasselled oats.

Gone, the rape-seed meadows midas-touched,
Crushed, the mottled plover eggs truant-clutched.
Soon the summer is but smouldering stubble;
Sad, when drystone walls decay to rubble.

Malcolm Williams

THOUGHTS FROM THE FOREST

Dark lowering trees, the forest's guard, to
watch you on your way.
Dark waiting hills, no welcome there, go stranger,
do not stay.
Dark watchful eyes, whose cold bleak look
says all there is to say.

Joan Warner

A WISTFUL MIRAGE

Blue sky and the drone of a bee
A calm and glistening sea
Lying idly on a grassy path
Eyeing with dreamy eye the golden thatch
Of a cottage across the way
Macs and wellingtons happily packed away
As summer heat touched her as she lay

But, alas, it was only in the beholder's mind
As she tentatively opened a jaundiced eye
Knowing only too well what she would find
Sea and a sky merged in doleful grey
Seagulls screaming after their prey
Not a soul to be seen . . .
A typical British summer's day!

C Leaper

SUMMER

The beautiful long summer days
they never seemed to end, just
went on and on, day after day
such carefree days, when no one
bothered to rush.
take your mind back now to reflect
on those lovely times when all was
calm and collected, it does not
seem so long ago, but oh, to
dream! Why not, life will pass
us by if we don't reminisce, then -
will we say, what happened to
those days, lazy, hot, unending
summer time, when we were young.
Let's dream some more.
Selective nights in our thoughts of
days gone by, look back now
while you may.

Pauline Ray

VISION

Sunlight melts into the sea, drifting Angels laugh with glee.
Ocean waves dance about, foam and spray hitting out.
Shattered rocks across the ground, loosely flattened by the sound.
Coarsely weaved weeds a trust to the sky in a gust.
Floating aimlessly through the swirl, needing reason to resolve.
Swollen banks where waters lie, child asleep on the rye.
Dreams just gone to a magical place, taken by a boat of lace.

Petra J Watkin

BLUEBELLS ON LYTH HILL

High up on Lyth Hill,
    where magic is silent,
And bluebells spill,
    in abundance.

For carpets of blue,
    with an April flower,
To the woods they plough,
    a magnificent power.

Yet trodden and flodden,
    'Make haste, make haste!
It is almost autumn,
Shall by then be chaste!'

But 'Neh! Give growth!'
    To this shadowy abode,
'tween the trees,
    where alliance doth
Grow a mellowing breeze.

Jamesina le Strange

HEATHLAND COTTAGE

There it stood in thirties years,
But now forever gone.
A heathland cottage painted white,
And roses round the door.
The whicket gate to heathland led,
All heather, broom and gorse.
The far horizon one could see,
And wondered, what beyond.

The larks in flight would all delight,
And siskins nesting there.
A butterfly with wings of blue
Danced on the heathland hue.
Linnet, goldfinch, curlew,
Were seen up in the sky.
For Nature's beauty dwelleth there
Upon the peaceful scene.

Farewell to heather, broom and gorse,
And cottage painted white.
History writes their destiny,
When wartime roar of aeroplanes.
Across the heath will fly,
There, pilots train to liberate
The lands across the sea.

In my dreams again I see
A cottage painted white,
And roses red around the door.
The whicket gate to heathland leads,
All heather, broom, and gorse.
A far horizon there I see,
And wonder, what beyond *prees heath.*

M L Dawson

HEREFORDSHIRE BEACON

You can stand on top the Beacon
With good views to either hand;
To the east you see the Cotswolds,
To the west Welsh table-land.
The Evesham plain is flat and green,
With rivers running through.
The Ledbury hills are gentle mounds -
An undulating view.

The patchwork fields are lush, or bare,
According to the season.
The trees add differences, too:
In leaf, or not, the reason.
At times you see ten miles or more -
It can be only one.
You pick out landmarks that you know,
Spot-lighted in the sun.

Around your feet the flowers grow -
Daisies, heathers strew the ground;
Bluebells, rose-bay, primroses.
Birds, in paradise, abound.
Small animals can roam at will.
You sometimes see a deer.
There's butterflies, moths, insects too.
Where ever else like here?

B J G Maitland

FOREVER FREE

S outh West of England
O h! To find,
M ore beautiful country yet,
E vergreen pastures,
R ugged hills
S teeped in history, least we forget,
E ternal springs and rivers flow
T hrough gorges deep and far below.

Pat Drew

UNTITLED

Gliding in silky waters, while the sun continues to shine -
The grass banks explode into full moons of colour.
The feel is so sublime.

Fluffy, wide-eyed bodies, watch where I go -
As I float downstream - going with the flow.

Then comes the night, with dark -
Until a new day dawns with the singing of the lark.

Debra Neale

SPIDERS

Spiders climbing up
your back
hey Jack up
your back

Climbing up the
bedroom walls
sneaking through the
kitchen door

When I climb into
the bath
all I see is legs
of black

When it comes to
the night
all they do is
give you a
fright.

Zoe Stevens (12)

SHROPSHIRE CLOUDS

You should see the clouds
In *Shropshire*, billowing white,
Like big pillows
In the blue sky.
How fast those clouds go by.
Catch them if you can!
Here's a fish, a polar bear,
Ready to pounce, look there!
Who needs pictures in the fire,
Or a TV set.
Pictures in the sky
Are better yet!

M Whitsitt

THE KING

The lion is the king of all,
One swipe of his fist,
And he will make you fall,
He is fast when he springs,
With his feet like wings,
When home to his young,
With their food he brings.
There he's a softy and likes to play
And covers his young to hide them away
In soft grasses like hay,
To protect them from other beasts of prey.
He is clever and crafty
And knows when you're there,
So watch out, he will see you.
And there might be a pair.

Shirley Rowland

SHROPSHIRE

On Shropshire's softened rolling plain
Of ancient fields of corn and rape
Wind sweeps o'er the fallen remains
Of heaving oak blown out of shape.

From emerald hills of Wales there glides
The Severn chestnut waters stare
On Severn Bore where history rides
O'er meadows washed with Marches air.

Below the Wrekin's clinging wood
Shadows creep o'er Wroxeter's spheres
Stones echo from where Romans stood
Well washed and worn with English tears.

Fox hunting to the poacher's beat
Long Mynd thunders to horses hooves
Clee Hills covered by snow white sleet
Wenlock Edge and valley grooves.

Below castle and market town
Looking west to Celtic towers
Above memory creek left to drown
To Offa's Dyke blushed with flowers.

Hamlet's pucker at fresh run streams
Much Wenlock, Acton, Stretton stone
Love songs and flitter of their wings
To hillside copse these birds have flown.

Shropshire plain ingrained with history
Reach out from heath to every shire
Castles and medieval mystery
Rivers, village and fields of mire.

M C Evlyn-Bufton

THE BEACHCOMBER

Seagulls flying overhead
Go unnoticed, as with eyes searching
The sea washed beach
I wander to and fro
Stopping only to pick up and gaze
In wonderment at the shapes
And colours of the shells and pebbles
To be found there
Gazing into rock pools
There is life in abundance
Crabs scuttling to and fro
Limpet shells tighten their grip
On their own special piece of rock
Star fish bask in sun warmed waters
Waves lap gently on the shore
Tangled heaps of seaweed lie
Dried up and discarded near by
Driftwood angled and smoothed by the waves
Is strewn along the water's edge
Every day a changing scene
As tide and current wash it clean

Valerie Sharp

NIGHT TIME IN OLD SOMERSET

The patchwork quilted landscape blurs its edges
And shadows shroud the interwoven hedges.
Stone mullioned windows watch the day's descent
Into the darkening hours of discontent.
A virgin vixen screams beyond the hill
And predator and prey alike are still.
Time holds its breath, as silence casts its spell,
Then whispers through the woods that all is well.
Where moonlit branches, generations high,
Stand out, stark skeletoned against the sky.
And bracken framed, a natural vignette
The blundering badgers' two toned silhouette.
Close quartered cattle huddle in their stalls,
And country colours fade as twilight falls.
The heavy headed shires stamp fretful feet
As cruising cats patrol their private beat.
Unseen by lingering lovers, self engrossed,
The spectral owl, a streamlined silver ghost.
A collie twitches in uneasy sleep
One ear on sentry duty for his sheep.
The stockpot simmers, spitting, on the grate
The longcase clock records the passing date.
Whilst simple folk, with secret dreams unguessed
Lie undisturbed by midnight's sweet unrest.

Jenny Holmes

IMPRESSIONS AFTER AUTUMN

With the sun over one's shoulder
Yesterday's silver birches are purple
Against the golden bracken.
An outcrop or occasional boulder
Breaks the continuity; rich browns slacken
To pallid greys in rabbit runs of pounded turf.
Gorse bushes, still dotted and defiant
With yellow blossoms, rally
Together in dark waves like bunching surf,
Saving appearances in the Green Alley
Where otherwise, despite bright ribbons of grass,
The reality is hardly a festival of spring.
The Sugar Loaf, one of so many,
Peeps over an accommodating pass
Beneath the treeless Beacon, a giant
By these standards, as gaunt as any,
And in gloomy silhouette, intimidating.

But now the horizontal sun
Tops the hill's companion with a cap of light
That dares the eastern plain to fade away
In shadow. It does too, as anyone
Who knows the game of heaven and earth
Can tell; the way things are, the night
Must come sooner on the sheltered side, while day,
Which lingers on perversely, knows its new birth
Will be later in the west. It comes first
On Bredon, surprising its crown of cloud
Sometimes by breaking the top free,
The solid centre emerging to burst
Into solitary confinement, its crowd
Of followers left straggling confusedly.

And often it leaves last in layer on layer
Of quilted mist, pink threads disturbing the shroud
But promising tomorrow's eternity
As the noble gift of humble prayer.

Stewart Richards

DECEMBER NIGHT IN MALVERN

Pale blue lights shivering
As if they were stars dipped in the navy blue sky,
And scattered in the valley
Now mingling with the gold
From street lamps.
The Priory bells ring out for Christmas
They say -
There is a God
There is a God
He's come
He's come -
Where?
An old tree, half broken
With black empty branches
Dips into the valley,
Digging the sky,
Reaching down towards the Priory
Which shines symbolic -
Cosy, replete with God.
Another God pulls the tree
Lower, and lower into the valley,
Then releases it
Her almighty arms move up the hillside
Pulling the trees back
The Priory bells keep calling -
It's just the wind
It's just the wind
That's all
That's all -
They are not moved

Janet Palmer

COUNTRY DELIGHTS

Sleepy village, quiet and still,
Close by a stream, set on a hill.
Church and mansion built to last,
Reviving memories of the past.

Across the meadow, through a gate,
Some of Nature's joys await.
Along a path beside the stream,
Lace winged damsels brightly gleam.

Summer's drought and lack of rain,
Has changed the stream to near a drain.
In shallow pools lined with sand and clay,
Bright eyed fry, they swarm and play.

Swiftly following stream's winding bed,
Kingfishers flash, in blue and red.
Dark humped back herons flap and flop,
As slowly on their spindly legs they drop.

High above the leafy trees,
Kestrel hawk, he glides and weaves.
Soaring high then circling low,
To strike his prey with deathly blow.

Browsing in a secluded glade,
The dappled deer seemed unafraid.
Until they caught the watcher's scent,
Then, heads held high, away they went.

In the pine trees coos a dove,
Singing his sweet song of love.
Now it is the turn of day,
And no longer, can we stay.

Lionel A Roebuck

A WINTER WALK ON COPPETT HILL

Sometimes there is no choice, I have to walk.
Perhaps these solitary days are best, a quicker pace, more room to think.
Now this is all I want, this view, this morning now.
The silver ribbon coils its way around the hill,
Shining in early sunlight. The hardest frost makes crystalline
The leaves and grass, to crunch beneath.
The sudden view to westward, turning at the climb,
The Sugar Loaf, the Skirrid, there gleams Wales,
And all the fields lie veiled in white beneath.
Behind, the Malverns, nearer Chase, Howl Hill,
Enjoying unexpected warmth, alive with birds.
Below, the sandstone castle, Goodrich, shines.
The magic place. Its chapel teems with ghosts.
Beside the folly I catch breath. Three buzzards glide.
The Yat crowns all, the guarded gate. The air is glass.
Above the ferns the path leads on along the top,
Past Jelemy's Tump, untouched by sun, then through a dainty wood
Of coppiced beech. A squirrel, jay, a nuthatch.
Now downwards to the stile beneath the Coldwell rocks.
The grass is petrified, untouched, my steps alone.
Under the crags the heather textured wall,
The purple catkins, ivy, old man's beard.
No peregrines in sight, but eight black cormorants sit there,
In contemplation, yellow beaks towards the sun.
The river swollen, banks eroding still.
The path is different every time I come,
And so am I. But I will tread this coppiced walk
And wonder at the gift alone.

Ann Elliott Wall

OUR HERITAGE

Our quiet village steeples,
Filled with many varied peoples,
Our rutted sprawling farms,
Tales of work and lucky charms,
Our meandering rivers in patchwork quilt,
Lost in time with grime and silt,
Our orchards blossom a carpet of colour,
Pink and white compliment each other,
Our seasons return with warm regularity,
Let us not forget this time - you and me.

Darren Martin Williams

AUTUMN

Ditches decide to be rivers,
Spilling across the late autumn roads.
Like a ship, the library van sails through the floods,
Making waves that upset a few lost ducks,
Halting for squirrels, who don't see why they haven't
got the right of way -
Gathering nuts is far more important!

And the farmers mend fences to prepare
for the onset of more storms,
While the talk is of harvest festivals and
The WI raid all the dried flower books.

Pushing through the branches which hang
in cascades of autumn gold from the canopies of trees,
like myriad tunnels, whose ends are unknown.
Ploughing through the country lanes with sunlight
like lightning, catching the red and yellow leaves,
sending them like flames,
darting in the breeze, beneath the wheels of the van.
This crazy glow of life, like candle light
flickering brightly before
the death of winter.
People, part of all the nature I travelled through,
bowing in the sadness of imminent dying, crying
with the death of the leaves, as
the souls of those they love, fall also
with the end of autumn.

Ann Hart Knight

MY WINTER FRIEND

My snowman looks so lonely
Bearing wild winter chills
In a gentle fall of early season snow
With a half bristled broom
Placed neatly through his arm
A perfect resting place for a crow

While a robin sings a sweet song
From a rooftop nearby
And a pine tree stands alone across the way
Where a squirrel dashes freely
To the top from bough to bough
Clutching goodies that will keep him through the day

He stands with a warm expression on his face
With his carrot nose and eyes of shining coal
And odd dimpled patches
That have formed on his arms
Where the rain erodes away into a hole

In the morning he'll be gone like the robin
As will the squirrel that ran freely in the tree
And all that will remain of my dear winter friend
Will be the carrot nose, the coal his hat and me.

Lynda Dolphin

LOOK NO FURTHER

Out of the city, and into the peace
Where animals roam, with the wind in the trees.
The air is so fresh, it makes me smile
Whilst field upon field, make a patchwork of miles.

Amongst brambles in ditches, some flowers all bough
And over a hedge looks a very fine cow.
Spread at his feet, is a carpet of green
Look to the corner, for the freshest of streams.

A farmer is ploughing and planting his crops
There's barley and maize, and plenty of hops.
With orchards of apples, a cider maker's dream
And rivers with salmon, pike and some bream.

No-one can know the country so well
Than the people who live there with tales to tell.
So Hereford people get out and about
As beauty surrounds you, without any doubt.

Pat Potter

TO GLEAN GRASS

We are still walking
Mournful as the dirt
Along this road lying hard underfoot,
Niggling like a half heard whisper,
Thinking of a voice in the sky,
But no blue sky is emanating
Over all these houses
Around our shivering heads . . .
No blue in the air
Lightening us, like a wave of hair
And no sun gleams.
And no grass underfoot
Squeaks and crumbles silently
No ingrained fertility calms our tread.
The road leads up and up
As steep creeps the hill
As though feet were held in lead
Quartering their sap.
Two miles has gone by.

A green field appears in sight . . .
The heads start dancing,
Prancing, waking legs and feet
To wend through fields of grassy green as seen
Which lies, melting under puny feet
Inspiring thoughts as rich and soft as its sheen.

J E Fowler

COLOURS OF HEREFORDSHIRE

Spring arrives with daffodils yellow,
Bluebells bright and primroses mellow;
White apple blossom bubbling like foam
In orchards grown on rich brown loam.

Summer follows with sheep in White Lemster Ore,
Rolling green valleys from Ross to Abbeydore;
Bright yellow fields and trees in full leaf,
Red and white cows bred for Herefordshire beef.

Autumn creeps slowly with robes of rich hue:
Gold leaves falling gently on the early morning dew,
Silver hoar frosts glisten in the watery sun,
Ruby red berries warn of cold weather to come.

Winter passes quickly, brown trees moan their song,
Old Man's Beard fills the hedgerows along;
Bright holly green and mistletoe white,
Only the robin can be seen in flight.

So Hereford's seasons roll peacefully by,
Each one nourished by the gentle blue Wye;
And God's promise of hope in the colours of the bow
Is ever present as the years ebb and flow.

Caroline Wood

DEVON'S COUNTRY LANES

Take a walk down Devon's country lanes,
Look at the beauty that can be found.
Open your eyes so you can see,
The things today, rare, but used to be.

Deep rutted cart tracks with grass between,
High sided banks of browns and green.
Flowers of blue, yellow, pink and red,
This is the jewel of nature it is said.

Under the tunnel of the hazelnut trees,
Full of flowers where soon nuts will be.
Past hedges with bramble and roses entwine,
Destined to be the colour of wine.

Thatched cottages under oak trees stand,
White painted walls the work of man.
Adding to the beauty of the fields and trees,
The song of the birds, the buzz of the bees.

Beside the track a small stream flows,
Under the bridge and away it goes.
Nourishing all nature along its way,
Bubbling and tumbling night and day.

Animals along the track are found,
Living above or below the ground.
Big or small they all live here,
In the past had little to fear.

Man destroys all in its way,
The plants, birds and animals have no say,
Devon's country lanes will soon be gone,
Is this to be a last swan song.

P B Ford

QUEEN OF THE RIVER

When rowing up the river
Ripples on the water
Admiring the wildlife
Keeping an eye on his daughter.

Then, almost effortlessly
Appears a beautiful sight
Graciously ruling the river
Her plumage, bright white.

Her head held high
Adorned with a glistening crown
Meticulously cleaning
As she glides into town.

When her young are born
Colours of brown and grey
Errr those ugly ducklings
You may hear people say.

When they grow older, a transformation
occurs
From grey to sparkling white
Queen of the river
Such a magnificent sight.

Robin Woolgar

SEASCAPE

When the gusty winds of autumn cleave the air,
And the seas roll swiftly in across the strand,
White-horses toss their flowing manes in glee,
Flinging the dark green weed toward the land.
I breathe the heady tang with eyes tight shut,
And lick my lips that taste of salt and sand.

Turning I fight my way along the front,
To find a sheltered seat on which to rest
And watch the waves their fearsome rite perform,
The snowy spume rides high upon each crest,
A pounding rhythmic roaring fills my ears,
My thoughts dissolve, my mind with sleep obsessed.

I dream I am a child again,
The gentle wavelets lap around my wriggling toes,
My father's hand in mind, I jump and shriek,
'The sea's so big, I wonder where it goes?'
'All round the world and never never stops,'
He answers me, and strokes my upturned nose.

Awakening then, I feel refreshed,
The wind is dropping and the clamour fades,
But still the waves their ebb and flow repeat.
So like the sea is life, with all its changing shades,
How very dull without that it would be,
Smiling at this, I turn for home, and tea.

Freda E Allen

MASTER AND SERVANT

When Reuben ruled our churchyard,
With hook and scythe - and time,
The toughest grass between the graves
Found that growing was a crime!
And seeds and weeds, even trees
- Especially that old elm
Seemed to grow in season and in reason
And dared not overwhelm.
But, when Reuben's granite stone was raised
- Beneath the elm (as he had said)
Then grass and weeds burst into life,
And the elm alone is dead!

John Steele

WILD SEA ROVERS

We are sons, of the wild sea rovers
The tribe of the sea, fish drovers
We see our fathers, set forth, some times never

to return

But still the waves we never spurn
Our summer spent lingering, by the tide
Mending our fish nets, until our next ride
We survey, the deep cruel ocean
Watching with eager eyes, we scan
The dancing waves, upon the shore
The desire to ride the waves once more
The sea to us is a woman
Whose beauty, lures and attracts every man
Whose smile lures, the sailors and ships

forth to sea

But the fury, of her angry waves, we do not see

Denise Walker

GARDENING MY WAY

How beautiful it is to
hear the blue-tits singing
and the beautiful displays
of tulips and crocus. And
the beautiful lily of the
valley. Honeysuckle blossom
climbs the walls and fences
people passing by on foot
admiring the display.
Having good neighbours
cheers us all up with their
smiles like the cheerful
face of the pansy blowing
in the wind.

Alan Hattersley

BEAUTIFUL BRITAIN

The Scottish Highlands, the Yorkshire Dales,
Over the border we go into Wales.

Valleys and mountains, breathtaking views,
Warm sandy beaches to run without shoes.

Off down to Devon, pass by the tors,
Travelling by the desolate moors.

Cruel rocks of Cornwall with picturesque bays,
White foam from the sea catching sun's rays.

Come to the Cotswolds, with villages quaint,
Artists have captured their beauty in paint.

Visit the cities, cathedrals so fine,
Majestic and regal, of perfect design.

Lakes, lochs and rivers, burns, fells and springs,
Each play a part with the beauty it brings.

Historic castles proud of their past,
Over the centuries their splendour will last.

Flowers of the Scillies, the Needles of Wight,
The island of Skye, a tourist's delight.

Round and about us these glories are seen.
Oh! God has blessed Britain, country supreme!

Sheila D Hanman

IN THE APE HOUSE AT BRISTOL ZOO

Behind the barriers and screening glass
The curious throngs of Homo Sapiens pass.
Derision or distaste by some are shown
For these gross shapes, though kindred to their own.
Most, fascinated gaze.
But Jill, unheedful both of interest or jest,
Cradles a sleeping baby to her breast
Entranced in contemplation of this treasure,
The son of her old age.

Now, in full measure,
Here at this dim-lit cage a watcher could
Behold the shining joy of motherhood
And its transforming power.
Arms that could prodigies of strength perform
Gently enfold the little clinging form.
Hands that could wrench a stanchion from its place
With feather touch fondle his tiny face,
Lips that in livid rage could spit and hiss
Nuzzle, caress and kiss
In ecstasy of bliss.

'She *loves* it mummy! Look!' A small voice cries,
And those who linger here will glimpse perchance
Something of the Madonna in that awkward stance
And the rapt worship in an orang's eyes.

Mollie Gosnold

MY PLOT

My plot is small, no rambling grand estate.
I have no bailiff, or lodge beside my gate;
No peacocks wandering idly on my lawn,
Nor deerherd; - no, not a single fawn.
Not open to the public, but access to my friends
At any time at all, not only at weekends.

I have no woodland husbanded with care;
No sweeping gravelled drive; - nowhere
A fountain in the middle of a lake;
No summerhouse to sit in to have my tea and cake.
But there's a little corner where I can put my chair.
There's room for you as well, if you'll join me there.

There's no grand cedar tree that's very, very old;
But I have conifers of green and gold,
An apple tree and prunus - honeysuckle too,
Lavender and rosemary, - and roses, just a few;
A little clump of violets, bluebells in the hedge,
And pots and pots of daffodils standing on a ledge.

You won't find a conservatory full of swaying palms.
There's just a tiny greenhouse, and geraniums!
Nor will you find a dovecote, however hard you try;
You'll find a worn-out birdtable, hung up very high.
You'll see the birds that come there, knowing where to look,
And a string of peanuts hanging from a hook!

No herbaceous borders or big flower beds,
No bronze lions with crowns upon their heads,
Or rolling meadows in greens of different tones,
There's just a simple patch of grass crossed by paving stones.
But it's *my* little kingdom; my bit of real estate;
That special world that lies beyond my garden gate.

E M Summers

COUNTRY LANES

Shades of green have always been the beauty of this land
Not intended and not foreseen was their departure from God's plan
Sending the birds and the animals of the greenbelt into a daze
Foraging around choking from the fumes of a carbon monoxide haze
Remembering how there were once better days
How their ancestors lived peacefully without the intrusion and
destruction
The hustle and bustle of these here motorways
Are these to be the country lanes of our future?
Is the M25 the new scenic route?
Has the song of the lark been replaced by a hooter
Are concrete and tarmac nature's new recruit?
If in using the word progress we mean to achieve for the better
then it's really a question of for who
Certainly not for the wildlife who constantly chant
'What have we ever done to you?'
Well I'm afraid the belt has come undone and the green
slipped down
Meanwhile more trucks and tractors help to
demolish and lay hot tar upon the ground.

Steve Sayers

APPLE BLOSSOM

Blossom - fragile and freshly bunched and thick,
Closely white-cusped on every branch -
Your petals are for the rain to pick,
Your pollen free for bees to take.

Blossom beauty cripples fast:
These cool clusters soon will break
And this year's spring be of the past
But what exquisite thing can last?

Wilfred J Plumbe

SONNET - BEECHY BUCKS

A leafy lane that wanders to a hill,
And finds a path to take me through a field:
Then by this way ascending yet, until
Beneath the shade of beeches there concealed
A fairyland within a woodland dell.
A blanket of bluebells arrests my view:
An azure sea, a glimpse of sky, to dwell
O'er shadowed by the beech trees' verdant hue,
Beyond the wood upon a nearby hill,
My eyes delight now with a rural scene:
A vale of Chiltern lowland - lying still.
With villages and hamlets in between.
Then morning mists began to disappear,
And revealed the peace of Buckinghamshire.

Jack Judd

CAUSE AND EFFECT

The Motor-way has halved the land
And from the north-side hill I view
Where hedgerows grew, railed fences stand
Misshapen fields and farm tracks new.

A patch-work quilt - this rustic scene.
Soft corduroy of fresh ploughed land,
Edged by an unploughed braid of green,
Velvety stripes, some chalk, some sand.

Alongside, taffeta shot with greens,
Young corn shoots - fine blades of grass,
Changed by the light and angle seen
As shadows of the clouds rush past.

Dragon-flies dart as insects pass.
The hovering Kestrel stoops 'ere long.
Starlings in dying branches mass,
And traffic noise drowns skylarks' song.

Gone are the lanes where violets were found.
Where hedge and bank were trimmed each year by hand.
Fast moving cars and lorries now abound
The motorway has scarred our peaceful land.

Peggy Fountain

AUTUMNAL BUCKS

A harvest patchwork spreads across the land,
From palest straw to darkest deep-turned earth,
With here and there a grazing green of fields
And ditches dug for winter's muddy floods.
A yellow leaf turns gently through the air
While berries ripen in the reddening hedge;
Below, the grass lies faded, wispy-dry.
The sun-bleached stalks of withered summer weeds
Stand stiffly in the straggling uncut verge,
Cadaverous spectres of the richer days.
      Another summer slips beneath the soil
      To join the million summers rotting there
Where death and darkness feed the hidden growth
Of yet another Spring - Persephone!

Diana Good

POOR BUCKS?

No mountain high, no highland tor,
No craggy peaks where eagles soar.
No fathomless mere, no rugged coast,
No heather moor can 'poor' Bucks boast.
But wait, just seek and you will find
Much beauty of a different kind.
Lush meads where listless rivers glide
With creaking willows on either side,
Pausing oft at silent mills
Where mighty water-wheels stay stilled,
Bluebell woods can still be found
Where oak and ash and beech abound.
Ancient hedgerows still in place
Make country lanes so fair of face.
Quaint villages display a need
For thatcher's deftness with the reed.
Aloft the lark sings sweet at dawn,
And in the grass there lies a fawn.
Nor is this county far too flat,
The greatest myth of all is that.
Hills with wooded dell and crest,
Panoramic views that catch the breath.
Secret places where on favourite beech
Nightly the owl emits his eerie screech.
With great pride this inland shire
Displays her magnificent attire.
From earliest times this county fair
In England's history has played her share.
Great battles on her fields were fought
To depose a king the Roundheads sought.
Historic and beauteous to be sure,
Buckinghamshire is not really 'poor'

S Rosemary Ward

89

GREENS

How many shades of green are there in the Surrey countryside?
We use a single name - but the range of shades is wide.

There's the yellowish-green of the primrose leaf
In its neat and furry whorl;
And the pinkish green of poplar leaves
As they start to unfurl.

The lamb's ear, softly velvet
Has a greenish-silvery sheen
And the jagged leaves of the feverfew
Are an acid, limey, green.

The holly, which is blackish green,
In spring has bronze green tips.
The wild rose fruits are a brownish green
As they ripen into hips.

Conifers come in many hues
Of gold and blue-grey-green;
And hostas all display their leaves
In shades of greenish cream.

The new seeds of the honesty
Are a greeny-purple shade
And certain types of lichen
Glow in orange jade.

When September's dews chill the air
And summer is almost dead,
The green of the land is tinged with
A touch of rusty red.

So - how many shades of green are there?
The answer must be :
As many different shades of blue
As there are in the sky and sea.

Joan Densham

A CHILD'S PARADISE

St Albans park in the summer
Was paradise for me
The children would paddle, run and laugh
While the adults sat under a tree.
The picnic was ambrosia
Which we ate without washing our hands;
Before the adults had finished
The children were doing hand stands!

We bothered and badgered the adults
To take us to the swings,
We walked slowly past the tea rooms
Where they sold ice-creams and things;
At this point dad would challenge us
To a race - 'Last one's a twit!'
Dad was nearly always last
But he didn't mind a bit.

The ducks were always hungry
So we gave them all the crumbs,
And we laughed as the growing ducklings
Ran to catch up with their mums.
The bells in the Cathedral
Rang out their songs of joy
St Albans Park is paradise
For every girl and boy.

Lynn Thoume

THE SEVERN SPRING FLOOD (AYLBURTON)

The first of flood at equinox
Lays futile siege to feathered flocks
River-bed sanctuaries twice daily stolen
Brown swirling waters by nature swollen
Brown swirling water's aggressive mission
Takes proud sand islands to submission
So is the awesome Severn Spring Flood
Stir the heart, chill the blood
Within a lifetime quite everyone should
See once at least, a Severn Spring Flood.

In but one hour the basin fills
The tidal stream now overspills
River-bank sanctuaries twice daily stolen
Grey menacing water by nature swollen
Grey menacing water, rising ranging
Acres green to silver changing
So, is the awesome Severn spring tide,
Water's return to Britain's side
By relenting moon's Atlantic divide;
Lunar timescale's rhythmic spring tide.

Ian Bendall

WINTER

Telegraph lines hang
like frozen threads to a web,
the frost illuminates,
the misty essence of tears.
Dead shadows dwell,
like the last breath of summer.

Winter's a graveyard
of debt wrinkled corpses,
miles of greenery stand,
like carpets of milk.
children sliver and slide,
to the school gates made of snow.

Mat Duggan

POET'S WALK (CLEVEDON)

Striding up from the road on the path around the hill,
To pause and gaze to westward across the muddy pill,
Where small craft shelter from the falling ebbing tide,
And fishermen dig for bait by the still water's side,
Passing Kingston Symour's fields and pasture land,
Beyond to wooded Kewstoke, via sea, rock and sand.
Looking seaward to Holms flat and steep,
Their craggy mass to the water's edge do creep,
Past moors and inlets and the creeks romantic,
Onward the restless waves of the wild and wide Atlantic!

Up, down, around Wain's Hill we wander,
Spying St. Andrew's Tower yonder,
Nestling quiet in the fold of the hill,
Stands the old Norman Church, grey and still,
Guarding the graves the churchyard's possessed,
Where poets, artists and good Clevedon folk rest
And there to set slumbers dreaming,
The faint lap-lap of the channel streaming!

Meandering onward toward the bay,
Where Cleveden's Victorian town of grey,
Is resting on seven wooded hills,
Where ageing nostalgia abides and fills,
Now, the well-worn walk around the hill,
Is beloved by many and views that still
Please the eye and lift the heart,
For future folk this wish to impart,
Hoping all will enjoy the same sweet thrill,
As they too wander around the hill!

Joan D Clift

LOVE BIRDS

The field was full of little birds.
You opened the car door and stepped
Into the cold November air.
They flapped away, nothing was there.
My heart is full of little moments,
If you go through the door without me,
Into the falling fading rain,
They will disintegrate, and all the joy be pain.

I watched and waited for the birds.
They never came back,
Not even one.
They found another field, a brighter sun.
You came and sat beside me in the car
And lit a cigarette.
I watched the thin veil of its smoke,
The silence stretched until it broke.

You do not know the fear I have of you
Not being somewhere, always near.
Things go so easily that cost so much to gain.
Love seems the hardest to sustain.
In the car mirror, you catch my eye and smile.
Suddenly I am solid and secure.
Life is this moment, it is here and now.
And birds that fly away, return somehow.

Linda Elston

95

SWEET EARTH

Upon the beach the wavelets lap
And stormy breakers roar
There's thrift on cliff and gorse is gold
Upon the open moor
The fragrant rose is rambling wild
Upon the cottage wall
And sun is sinking, sunset red
In fiery orange ball
The fish is glistening silver specked
Within the babbling stream
And butterflies still hover
And bees still buzz and teem
Dear Nature, you abundant lie
With every dawning birth
So may we keep this peacefulness
And love our dear sweet earth.

Maureen Warner

OCTOBER FROST WEST WALES

This morning the mountains are luminous.
In those high depths, frost becomes mist, mist sky
invisibly. Silent earth steams gently
to leaden grey steel grey silver white clouds.
Thistledown and willowherb seed earthlight
into space, galaxies, the universe.

Once in the forest, unfrozen frost drips
from overhead beech and sycamore trees:
a southern thaw already, to rust red
orange brown green, the mountain's other side.

Fields steam fiercely behind high hedges,
as though in Iceland or New Zealand. Surely
the sun is nearer than Llandeilo
and warmer than Golden Grove. Frost lingers
only in scraps, patches, pockets, and at
journey's end. Colours condense to violet,
blue cranesbill, leafless, frosted to a bell.

Janet Dube

POET'S VALLEY - IN ANCHORITE

Teaming a stream a withering winter'd streams dream
Heavens emptying in bucket fulls momentarily ceases
Teasingly to a halt
Then from sky's lustrous vault you pour like an involuntary
Bodily emptying itself like a wild beast on to mother earth
Glistening whimsical clouds of white beckoning fluff
Take shapes of angelic angels, demons and fat cats
Never to be seen twice
All life run for shelter now, under umbrellas, roofs, giant
Leafs and each other -
Fresh paint runs and separates into its elements
And spilt sheets of oil glisten as if with the wink of an eye
Now reflect back into a prism of vibrant rainbowed hue
And spread like a virus across the tarmac.
Softly dug turfed maggot encased mud froths and bubbles
With the vigour and appearance of a pair of young lungs.
Pitted pavements and swollen banks burst with a vengeance
Through corroded cast iron drains, where beamish children
Faces laminated and button bright sail paper boats down
Bluebell drive, coke cans sticked twiglets too in the gritty
Rippled ride.
Cars looked freshly washed and cleaned, (until morning that is!)
Chubby women in pinnies charge like bulls up the garden path
Fag'ed lipped and head scarf'ed tearing their clean linen
Off the line, peg springs snap, fly and dart in the attack.
All huddle indoors now over roaring fires and hot stoves
Rubbing down with fleecy towels and wiping condensation from
Their terraced windows among complaints of the weather.

Heidi Newman

SOPHIA GARDENS

Trees - Darkening at twilight
As shadow'd lace on the skyline
Where a star -
Straying from height
Candles a fir tree
To light
The evening's creeping scar:

Trees -
Chestnuts, elms, oaks and beeches -
Their branches
Spearing The ice-blue air:
Some crinolined
Bow to the castle's spectral heap
Behind the protective keep
Of Cardiff Castle:

Sophia Gardens
Moody in day's fading light -
Pulse earthily into the furtive gloom
Of stealthy, river misted clouding -
Now redeemed by the beaming
Of the rising moon.

K M Daugela

THE GARW - OLD VALLEY, NEW LIFE

High in the valley, away from the town
Is the source of the Ogmore where it starts to trickle down;
Drawing life from the mountains, gaining new energy,
Meandering down on its way to the sea.
Mountains that are ageless, born before men
Spring forth with new life each day again.

Deep in the valley the villages grew
As the coal gave the people a job to do.
Generations of families gathered around
The source of their livelihood deep in the ground.
A valley with a purpose, a community for the town
Till the day that the Coal Board closed it down.

Death to the valley, the papers said:
What life could be left if the mine was dead?
No jobs and no money, no future in store
For the ones who remained with 'For Sale' on the door.
Many were leaving, so many had gone
The valley was dying and the mountains looked on.

Now in the valley the life has returned
For the ones who remained and the lessons they learned;
That a town needs its people, that a home needs a heart,
Not the ones that deserted and drifted apart.
There is hope in the valley and businesses new
For a new generation with jobs to do.
A Community Hall gives a purpose and pride
And a future for children that once seemed denied.

Alyson Mountjoy

END OF TIME

Leaves fall as through the woods I stroll,
Crisply crackly like crisps beneath
my feet they form a carpet on the ground.
I look up at the towering trees
Their arms entwine, stripping of all their glory.
The wind blows up and sweeps
the leaves as she goes whizzing by,
A robin sings, a snowflake falls
Like snowdrops from the sky,
They form a pattern on the leaves
then fade away and die.

M E H Hibbert

KENFIG POOL NATURE RESERVE

Here is the sound of a quiet afternoon.
When the air is warm and the sun shines high.
And birds sing and crickets croon
Above the water of the pool where the mallards fly.

Nodding dainty heads the orchids wild peep through.
The green of lucious undergrowth parted by duneberry bush.
And here and there amidst the dunes a pigeon is heard to coo.
And humming bees and dragonflies hover round the tall bullrush.

I love the summer walks I take upon an evening clear.
To Kenfig Pool Nature Reserve where wild life is not disturbed.
You'd never know that cars and road were anyway near.
And there's no such thing as litter for that habit has been curbed.

Jeannette Jones

THE NEW SCRUBBED FACE OF MID-GLAMORGAN

We are near enough to the sea
For seagulls to seek sanctuary,
From fierce winds rolling over angry waves
The seagulls feel safe in our hillside caves.

Right under my home was a deep, dank, dark mine,
There my Grandad scrapped his spine
Against the black diamond walls,
Soon to be turned into red hot coals.

Now it's gone, but in it's place,
Are houses like boxes, all with the same face?
The steamy, sweaty, whitetilecold Pit shower room, is now,
A Councillor's rather smart, crisp-new, brick red . . .bungalow!

I remember a giant wheel, far above my Mother's face,
Now that too is no more, replaced, by . . . space.

Yule-tide trees of every green hue,
line up on the hillside, queue after queue,
Sharp pine needles piercing the blue, grey or black sky,
How I would love to be an eagle, bird or butterfly,
To soar over the lid of Glamorgan's heartland
Far below me trees and grass, roll by,
Moulded by an abundant hand.

Merylrose de Sivyier

AN ODE TO THE ABER VALLEY

Green valley,
Nestling between mountains
Shrouded in mist. At times darkly,
Suddenly! Bathed in sunlight,
Revealing its beauty anew,
For sunlight makes things brighter,
Unexpected is the beauty of the valley,
Lifting the spirit anew!
Like the wealth of mineral hidden in its depths,
For which men slaved endlessly to retrieve,
Daily they did strive,
Hidden in the darkness,
Rarely seeing their valley in the sunshine,
Working on till day was done,
Warmth of spirit too was there,
Unexpected, hidden but everywhere.
Sadness, joy, warmth and care
People had it, it was there!
And I perceived it from the start,
It has a special place within my heart.

Gwendoline Jones

THE VALE OF MY YOUTH

The vale of my youth,
where as a child I played,
in the grass as tall as the Valleys.
Till the glowing orb of the sun,
like the day did fade.
Then home to my mother I dallied.

Where the glistening sea, whispered secrets to the shore.
Where the land was wild and free.
Where a man and a child
gathered cockles, hand in hand,
on craggy rocks, my father and me.

As the didicoys sang for wares
in the light of dawn.
The men trooped to work in the mine,
and the women chattered, over cobbled garden walls.
While white washing billowed on the line.

Those long cherished days
of my South Glamorgan home,
with fond memories, to be forgotten never.
Of my family and friends
and a country so fine,
will keep warm my Welsh heart forever.

S M Curran

DYFED, FOR ALL SEASONS

Come walk with me today
To stand and look and reason.
To stroll the paths and byways,
Enjoy each lovely season.

The Spring, its joy of birth,
Springing from the warm brown earth.
Summer days of sun and heat,
Must admit, walking sometimes hurts the feet.

But in the cool of night
We marvel at the wondrous sight,
The sunset now will give up soon
To the dreamy romance of the moon.

Now we come upon the fall,
The glorious colours of falling leaves enthral us all,
Standing, wondering why the reason.

Winter now in pure white glory,
Changing to gales and rain,
Everything seems to go awry,
But wait, soon it will be Spring again.

W M Hart

LOOK I AM MAKING ALL THINGS NEW

I'd like to paint a picture grand
Of all the beauty close at hand.
A perfect world in harmony.
And perfect people there will be.

A perfect child with lovely eyes.
A beautiful bird, up in the skies.
The flowers so perfect in full bloom,
To brighten up a lovely room.

A perfect night, its stars so fine
Leads into day, the sun to shine.
Remember too. I'd paint the sea,
Great dolphins, playing happily.

Fresh water lakes, and lovely streams,
Are all awaiting in my dreams.
So many animals I see.
Such perfect beauty, there for me.
And lots of time will be at hand,
To let me paint, a picture grand.

This is the prize, that God will give
To everyone, who wants to live!
In loyalty and thankfulness
A beautiful world of happiness.

If I could make my hand portray
God's perfect world to be.
I'd have a picture from my heart,
That you could share with me!

Gwladys Gahan

BEAUTIFUL ISLE OF ANGLESEY

Born in a paradise, here I will grow,
Too young to appreciate, the pace being slow,
But when I'm older, and had time to learn,
How precious this island, I'll always return.

No subways or underground, no race for the rats,
Feet firmly on the ground, no high rise flats,
A sea going heritage, in each family,
How precious this island, slave of the sea.

Beautiful Isle of Anglesey,
They come in their hundreds to be by the sea,
No need to change your currency,
No need to be able to say, Llanfair P G

Carpets of scenery, all within reach,
Always a stones throw away from the beach,
You choke in your cities, how can you survive?
Our clean windswept island will keep us alive.

Bill Jones

PEN LLEYN (LLEYN PENINSULAR) GWYNEDD

Where does beauty reign supreme?
Where everything is clean and green,
Where time stands still
And people dream
Where the days are long
And never seem
To change.
Where the fresh fish gleam
In the mountain's stream
And mackerel is the sea's rich seam,
Home grown gooseberries
With farm fresh cream.
Where people are friendly -
Never mean.
Where is this place, (some have never seen?)
It's the North West Coast of Wales -
The Lleyn.

Patricia Meakin

THE GREEN VALLEY OF THE USK A WALK WITH GOD!

Lush meadows green where daisies screen,
Blue violets from the sun's bright beam,
Burst forth the Lark whose wondrous cry,
Awakes the dipper swift to fly.
The angler stands with face upturned,
To where his dapped fly is spurned.
And turns he now as salmon bold,
Leaps free from silvered waters hold.
Eyes lifted now beneath the leaf,
Red spinner flicks its courtship brief.
And down the brook his snout appoised,
The otter barks at nature's joys.
Where willow leaf does quickly part,
King fisher see his blue black dart.
A miriad bars of green and gold,
As minnows dodge his black beaked hold.
Ah! Gentle ewe, your white flock scatters,
As blue jay from his hide-out natters.
Come scamper now you rabbit timid,
Here lurks the fox - his eyes red rimméd.
Now blue in the dell as clouds appeared,
Beneath the fern's most saged beard.
Come shake and blow your fragrant scents,
Where blue bells tinkling tones are lent.
Now stand we still with hushed breath,
We feel the rush of storm clouds pressed.
As gentle rain caress our face,
We feel the touch of God's great grace.
And all the wondrous scenes before,
Are lost in rainbow's magic awe.

David Taylor

HAFOD SPRING DAWN

Blue skies through still-leafless larch
Hint at things to come.
Grey clouds flee the saffron-silver sun,
That warms the stone-chill ground,
And light-dapples mossy mounds,
Cushioned on countless seasons lost-leaf litter.

Fine-feathers firs, growth golden-green,
On tips of layered emerald.
The myriad knot-eyed trunks thinly concealed,
Gaze sightlessly through the red needle-floored gloom.
Above, the lonely keening of a solitary kite,
Seeking its last year's soul-mate.

The torrent falls, rock-forked, foam fighting free,
Not calmed from winter's force.
Grey rocks and moss clad walls bind it to its course.
Fast fluid silence breaks into foaming sound
A grandoise elfin-mischief dance in praise of this wild ground
To shepherd in the spring.

The old mill, cottage now, rests by the whirling green-brown pool
Short grass, sheep-cropped.
Shelters a solitary blooming daffodil.
Earliest, first of a green-gold vale-filling cascade,
That gently and irresistibly forces back the shade,
Spring has come again.

G C Hockley

RIVER OF DREAMS

Oh enchanting Teifi
Cast your mystic spell on me
As you weave your way
Through mountain and valley
And into yonder sea.

I look into your crystal waters deep
Yet see only a face that is known to me
Your body swells and narrows and surges
And moves in time to rhythmic pulses.

Along your banks fortresses rise
Though time has dealt them a deadly blow
But your beauty still takes my breath away
Time has not swept your grandeur aside.

Salmon embrace your warm rocky path
Against your swirling tide they gracefully glide
Through waters calm and up falls they fly
Their silver bodies reflecting under blue skies.

A host of Coracles adorn your waterways
Casting their invisible lines in the noon day sun
Creating ripples that spiral into your silent depths
The silence only broken by the odd reeling in.

Anywhere I go and anything I do
I will keep the memory of you forever
For there is no other place on earth I will see
What it is the river Teifi has shown me.

Vanessa Morris

THE EARTH

The Earth tumbling away in its monumental rhythm,
Forever in its orbital splendour,
The creatures of the earth held by gravity force,
And yet not aware of its pace through space.

The sun and moon taking turns to play tricks on its movements,
And cast shadows of its beauty to outer space,
Through countless centuries it has seen history come and go,
Its crust has been the stage of every romantic rendezvous.

Its outer layer has seen every battle fought won and lost,
It can bathe in sunshine or raging storms,
The snows, frost and ice seem to enjoy its ever nearer movement,
It never waits for anyone to get off or get on.

If you die it still carries you, how you get there I don't know,
It keeps its own supply of air, to keep us breathing,
It is just one colossal, gigantic, ever rotating multi-million centrepiece,
Thrown in amongst the universe and its cosmic counter-balancing.

Do I love it? I have to, I don't know of anything better!
I think of its beauty in mountains, lakes, rivers, sand, flowers, etc,
                                   beauty untold and behold.
I love its secrets, in deep caves, caverns, seas and forests
I can live a thousand years and never really understand you.

Its seas and rivers never empty in its ups and downs,
Its constant rotating in its merry-go-round,
Its changing beauty throughout the year, in its never ending fashion.
Its rays from the sun in its glorious passion.

The tumultuous hulk swings in noiseless motion,
And on its back it carries every ocean,
For millions of years it has reigned in its awesome wonder,
I hope to God you never fall asunder.

John-Joseph Cusaok

IN THE GARDEN

My world is full of colour now the garden's in bloom.
Striking contrasts fill the patio,
spilling where there's room.
Hidden from strong winds,
a ballerina pirouette's on fragile stems,
The fuchsia's here to entertain
an audience of impatiens.
Begonia's,
Red and yellow,
Cascade from baskets in the sun.
Lobelia Sapphire,
Cloaks King Balcon,
The silken leafed geranium.
The scented evening primrose,
Subtle in moon light's glow,
Creates a tranquil atmosphere
for the weary soul.
Come into my garden,
here you will find rest.
For here within the garden,
The gardener's busiest.

R Ditchfield

THE DYING SUN

Behind the dark hills the warm sun is dying,
Stretching red fingers high up in the sky;
Softly and sadly the breezes are sighing,
Mourning the sun and the day, as they die.

The sun dies in glory with colours ablaze,
He fights for the daylight, scorning the night,
And lights up the sky with bright crimson rays,
As bravely defiant he sinks out of sight.

Although he's defeated, his brightness is glowing,
Touching the clouds with a blush like a rose,
But slowly the colours are fading and going,
And night comes a-creeping as the sun goes.

K Burston

POPPIES

A gust of wind blows suddenly,
sending a shiver across the wheatfield
as you stand, glistening wet from your morning's shower,
gathering up your petticoats -
wafer-thin and engine red,
tilting precariously in the breeze.
You ask for nothing and you cause no pain,
still you must constantly struggle against the ravages
of the winds and the rain
in order to keep your fragile flame alive.

Julie Pangrazi

THE NEWS TODAY

I made a change today and took a saunter,
Instead of pushing on my usual way.
The Gilford road and things that I encounter
Seemed just the same as any other day.

The beauty in the eye of the beholder
The poet saw so very long ago;
With opened eyes perhaps because I'm older
I now perceive all round a different glow.

The trees stand true and tall in their longevity.
The green in grass is now a deeper hue.
The birds are swirling round in feathered levity,
While man is striving still for something new.

The cattle in the fields are munching steadily.
Incurious eyes survey my passing by.
The clover sweetened grass they eat so readily,
Providing to my daily milk supply.

The sun and rain provide all nature's harmony.
Conjoined they illustrate a scene of peace,
But separated each will clash discordantly,
With burning sun, and floods that can increase.

With avid eyes the poor of many nations
Look longingly at rich folks super fare.
Both young and old are conflicts poor relations.
Each day brings deeper needs for all to share.

When crabbed age and youth are in contention
Each see the others stand with different view,
And holding on with firmer, stiff intention
Prepared to see the current battles through.

And looking now at history through the ages
It seems all humans react just the same,
Reflecting as we sadly turn the pages
On mankind failures pictured once again.

W J Mitchell

THE SPARROW'S REVENGE

I'm the small brown sparrow
What perches in your gutter
And sings to you so cheerfully
Despite your fretful mutter
I know it's only five a.m,
But I've been up for hours.
And so would you if you'd been with me
And sat through all night showers,
Crouching by the chimney pot,
Cold and soaking wet,
Trying to fluff me feathers up
What's sticking to me yet.
But here I am awaiting
Me meagre bit of crumb,
Which judging from your tone of voice
Is not about to come.
All right then! If that's how you feel
I'll sing louder still on Sunday,
And louder still and earlier,
When you have to go to work on Monday.

Edith Groves

119

THE WEATHER

Some like walking in the rain
Others sit inside and complain
When the weather is crisp and cold
Oh! What affect will it have on the old
Then sunshine starts to appear
And brightens up the year
The season changes, it's a lovely hot day
Summer is really on its way.
But still there's some it doesn't please
They now await a breeze
Can't folks just be content
With whatever weather is sent
Sad to say this never will be
We'll always moan at what we see
Yes I admit that includes me.

Merril Morgan

HOP PICKING IN BOSBURY

Houses, brick and lime-washed, drowse in afternoon sun.
The air is sharp, bitter as wormwood, heavy with hops.
Distant shouts cut through the palpable quiet.
The clatter of tractor-trailers echoes down the sleeping street,
Reverberating from ancient, sun-warmed walls.
The road is strewn with crushed bines.
Window-sills are thick with the papery bracts.

In hop-yards, behind neat cottage gardens,
Pickers strip the tenting green from wire and pole,
Leaving the leafy alleys naked and despoiled.
A few torn bines remain, marooned,
Like tattered flags of a former glory.

In farm sheds machinery roars and judders.
Hoists winch away the curtaining bines.
Parchment cones lie, delicate, on the kiln's drying-floor,
Or crushed, baled tightly in the sacking pockets.

Gently the September twilight deepens.
Tractors stop, generators fall silent,
Workers stumble home to waiting caravans.
The village sinks back to rural somnolence,
Drugged with the heavy scent of hops.

Jennifer Lynne Ardrey

CLOUD COUNTRY

Have you ever seen the country of clouds?
  It's a fascinating sight.
It seems to be at the edge of the world,
  In autumn's early light.

It has mountains and valleys, and islands
  In rivers and seas of gold.
But the tale of this wonderful country
  Can never fully be told.

For it changes from moment to moment,
  And always from day to day.
When the sun is high in the heavens,
  It has vanished all away.

W M Green

THE SEA

The sea is clear and fresh, fresh,
The waves are lapping onto the beach
Searching for something it's lost,
Whipping spray into my face, colouring
me, making me cool.

White horses are galloping into the shore,
crashing against a castle and knocking it flat.
A gull cries out, the sea answers its
call and seems to beckon,
The gull obeys and floats away into
the cloudy horizon.

Becky Ramsay-Smith (12)

RAIN

The rain beats down from leaden sky
Grey full clouds passing slowly by
Empty streets not a soul around
Pitter-patter the only sound.

The birds take shelter under dripping eaves
Bare the trees without their leaves
Life so quiet and still remain
Silent wait for blue skies again.

Daylight hours pass swiftly by
Still the clouds fill up the sky
Endless rain keeps beating down
Sodden wet the cheerless town

Afternoon hours bring no respite
Raining still far into night
Gloomy day no sunshine's ray
Little chance of brighter day.

Evening time the darkness spread
Softly softly does night time tread
Rain drops sparkle on night time lights
Patterns form bright crystal sights.

Through the night the sleeting rain
Weeping clouds as though in pain
Towards the dawn the skies turn blue
Sun rise hour a crimson hue.

New day is born a whole new scene
Sunshine strong where the rain has been
Birds peep out and people wake
Bright the start to the new day break.

L Draper

MONARCH OF THE SEA

Monarch,
Shouting, as a King
thunders horseless
to the boundary
of flint wastelands.
Flowing coffers spill jewels,
molten sun, fired by the sea.
This breathing Lord,
moving, heaving forward,
each murmuring wave enchanted,
is blossom-edged in rippling lace.
His cliffs are walls
that echo back sound,
rumbling, under blue ceilings,
waiting for the stars.
The day, His court,
lined with tapestries
woven by flying birds,
that hid in the spindrift
and rose from the water.
We the courtiers
bow deep in wonder.

Margaret Gibian

THE OAK TREE

One morning on a bright new day
I took my walk a different way
Down a country lane I strolled
Such beauty and peace I did behold
The trees were at their very best
They filled me with such happiness
But one in particular caught my eye
A very old oak with its head in the sky
Its trunk was so thick so knarled and so bold
It must be I thought a hundred years old
The leaves were so patterned and cleverly made
It was hard to believe that the tree was that age
I stopped to think what magic hand
Had made a tree so tall and grand
And from a little acorn seed
Such majestic beauty had been freed

Edna Hobday

THE FIR TREES OF ENGLAND

You fir trees of England,
Stately tall and splendid in your finery of green.
What beauty within your depths reach ever
Out and up for eager eyes to savour and see.

Whilst all around is madness, still you
Stand Sentry like, towering and guarding,
Giving those who pause to look
A feeling of tranquillity.

Within your huge bendy boughs you lovingly
Cradle and enfold the birds, who nestle deep
And roost in summer heat and winter cold.

How festive is your beauty when cold winter
Snow trails softly over each ferny bough.
You were created for days such as these,
When others around you stand. Dead-like
And bare, you in all your finery stand
Jewelled and triumphant
There's nothing to compare.

Evergreen,
Everstay your lovely willow way,
Ever to enchant all who dare to look
Your way.

Linda Caunter

INFORMATION

We hope you have enjoyed reading this book - and that you will continue to enjoy it in the coming years.

If you like reading and writing poetry drop us a line, or give us a call, and we'll send you a free information pack.

Write to

Anchor Books Information
1-2 Wainman Road
Woodston
Peterborough
PE2 7BU